# Real-Life Writing Activities

## Based on Favorite Picture Books

BY GLORIA ROTHSTEIN

SCHOLASTIC
PROFESSIONAL BOOKS

NEW YORK • TORONTO • LONDON • AUCKLAND • SYDNEY
MEXICO CITY • NEW DELHI • HONG KONG • BUENOS AIRES

DEDICATION

*To Ryan and Hale–*
*With Love*

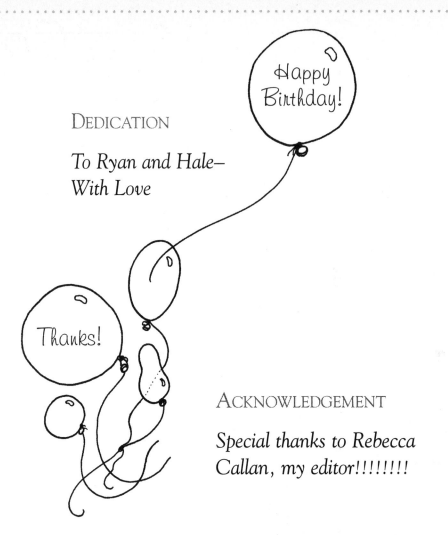

ACKNOWLEDGEMENT

*Special thanks to Rebecca*
*Callan, my editor!!!!!!!!*

Grateful acknowledgement is made to the following authors, publishers, and other copyright holders for permission to reprint the following covers:

From COOK-A-DOODLE DO! by Janet Stevens and Susan Stevens Crummel reprinted with permission of Harcourt Brace and Company. Copyright © 1999 by Janet Stevens and Susan Stevens Cummel.

From DEAR MR. BLUEBERRY by Simon James reprinted with permission of Margaret K. McElderry Books. Copyright © 1991 by Simon James.

From MISS SPIDER'S TEA PARTY by David Kirk reprinted with permission of Scholastic Press. Copyright © 1994 by David Kirk.

Cover design by **Norma Ortiz**
Cover and interior artwork by **Maxie Chambliss**
Interior design by **Holly Grundon**

ISBN 0-439-25616-X

4 5 6 7 8 9 10    40    09 08 07 06 05 04 03

# Contents

# Introduction

## Dear Reader,

**W**hat happens when Farmer Brown's cows get their hands on an old typewriter? *Click, Clack, Moo! Cows That Type.* Or when young Emily spots a whale in her backyard pond and writes to her teacher about it? *Dear Mr. Blueberry.* Can't you just picture a delightful note, letter, or message popping off the pages of these children's books?

Each time I pick up a children's book, even if I've read the title many times before, I'm looking for new ways to get kids more excited about reading and writing. So, flipping through the pages of *Lilly's Purple Plastic Purse,* I just had to ask, "Wouldn't students love the idea of writing little notes to Lilly and slipping them into her purple plastic purse?" Or, suppose I handed out printed invitations to join me for *Miss Spider's Tea Party?* Just think how many RSVPs I might receive!

Wouldn't students be more inclined to pick up pencil and paper if they were writing letters, notes, postcards, invitations, or clever messages? And how about these same children getting into the habit of making lists, taking telephone messages, jotting down recipes, and writing in diaries or journals? Putting books into the hands of young children helps to make them lifelong readers. Perhaps, by starting off with what many kids consider fun writing activities, we just might turn those kids into lifelong writers, too!

*Gloria Rothstein*

# How to Use This Book

To help you teach students how to write letters, postcards, notes, journal entries, lists, and more, 22 picture books have been carefully selected as models for teaching 11 kinds of writing in the classroom.

You'll find many of these popular books in the school library and on your own bookshelves. When, how, and in what order you use the read-alouds is up to you. While the simpler picture books may be more suitable for beginning writers and other titles more appropriate for your older readers, any one of these stories make great creative-writing prompts.

## What's Inside

Each featured picture book comes with activities that take you from introducing the book right through to extensions.

### A Story Summary: A brief synopsis of the book with key details you can use as you develop lesson plans.

### The Reading & Writing Connection: Before-reading questions for students that help spark interest in the links between reading and writing.

### Write Away: After-reading activities that use the story as a springboard for teaching a specific format of writing and eliminating those frequently asked questions: *What should I write about? Who should I write to? Where should I begin?*

### Reproducible Stationery: Illustrated writing paper designed to complement each picture book's theme and provide support for students as they practice writing notes, invitations, postcards, diary pages, lists, how-to's, recipes, messages, telephone messages, and more.

### Write Ideas: Extension activities you can use to reinforce the reading/writing connection. And since many stories inspire more than one kind of writing, you'll find a variety of writing extensions. For example, a read-aloud in the Invitations section might also generate interest in making a guest list, writing a message on a birthday card, taking a telephone message, or jotting down a party recipe.

### Another Great Model for Writing: More fun-to-read books you can use as springboards for teaching real-life writing.

# Links to the Language Arts Standards

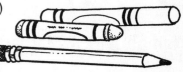

The National Council of Teachers of English (NCTE) and the International Reading Association (IRA) have collaborated and proposed what K–12 teachers should provide for their students to grow proficient in language arts. The writing activities in this book support these standards and help students to:

Read a wide range of print and non-print texts to acquire new information.

Read a wide range of literature from many periods in many genres.

Apply a wide range of strategies to comprehend, interpret, evaluate, and appreciate texts.

Adjust their use of written and visual language to communicate effectively with a variety of audiences and for different purposes.

Employ a wide range of strategies as they write and use specific writing process elements appropriately to communicate with different audiences for a variety of purposes.

Apply knowledge of language structure, language conventions, media techniques, figurative language, and genre to create, critique, and discuss print and non-print texts.

Use written and visual language to accomplish their own purposes.

These standards have been adapted from NCTE and IRA's Web sites:
http://www.ncte.org     http://www.reading.org

# Dear Mr. Blueberry

by Simon James (Margaret K. McElderry Books, 1991)

During a school vacation, Emily thinks she sees a whale in her backyard pond. So this imaginative little girl immediately writes to her teacher, requesting information about whales. Thanks to Mr. Blueberry, Emily learns some basic facts about whales, nature, and letter writing.

From the postage stamp on the front cover to the envelope seal on the back, this read-aloud offers a delightful way to introduce students to the importance of letter writing. *Dear Mr. Blueberry*, told through a series of letters, is the perfect letter-writing opener.

# The Reading & Writing Connection

Ask your students if they've ever written a letter to a teacher.

✳ When did you write it?

✳ Were you asking for information or advice?

✳ Has a teacher ever written you a letter?

✳ What kind of information did your teacher share with you?

## AFTER-READING ACTIVITIES

# Write Away

Make a copy of the letter stationery on page 10 for each child, and have students try a few of the following writing activities.

## A Letter to Mr. Blueberry

Emily writes letters to Mr. Blueberry asking for information about whales. Have students write a letter to Mr. Blueberry asking for information about an animal, bird, or insect they saw in their yard, on the way to school, or on the playground. Encourage children to tell Mr. Blueberry exactly what they want to know. Suggest they ask a specific question.

## A Letter to Emily

Mr. Blueberry writes letters to Emily telling her what he knows about whales. Invite students to write a letter to Emily telling her what they know about goldfish, turtles, hamsters, or other small pets. Ask children to share one or two interesting details with Emily. Encourage them to be specific.

## A Letter to Arthur

Emily reads one of Mr. Blueberry's letters to her whale, Arthur. Just for fun, have students write a letter to Arthur. Ask children to share some news about Emily, Mr. Blueberry, or themselves.

## P. S.

Emily put a P.S. at the end of her letter. So did Mr. Blueberry. Ask students to write a P.S. at the end of one of their letters. First, have them choose a letter. Then, encourage them to decide what they want to say.

_____

(date)

Dear _____,

_____

_____

_____

_____

_____

_____

_____

_____

_____

P.S. _____

Real-Life Writing Activities Based on Favorite Picture Books    Scholastic Professional Books

# Write Ideas

## A *Dear Mr. Blueberry* Stamp

**E**very letter needs a stamp! Have students create a stamp for one of the letters in this book. Ask them to decide which letter was their favorite. Tell them to imagine what they want their stamp to look like. Have children work with crayons, colored pencils, markers, and cut paper to design the stamps.

## A List for Emily

**T**hanks to Mr. Blueberry, Emily learned some facts about whales. As a group, compile a list of what children learned. Encourage students to name specific information they discovered about whales. See how many facts they can list.

## A "Dear Teacher" Mailbag

**E**mily wrote letters to her teacher. Why not have your students write letters to you! Print your name in colorful letters on the front of a large brown grocery bag. Hang this paper mailbag in a corner of the classroom. Tell students that you love to receive mail. As an ongoing activity, invite children to write you letters and drop them in your sack. Suggest that children ask for information or share news about things they see or do.

Writing
**Tip**

Remind students to sign their names to their letters.

# The Gardener

by Sarah Stewart (Farrar, Straus & Giroux, 1997)

During the Depression, while her parents are out of work, Lydia Grace Finch is sent to the city to live with her Uncle Jim, a baker who never smiles. This young girl, who happens to love gardens, sets off on her own with a suitcase full of seeds and some stationery. Although she knows a lot about gardens, she knows nothing about baking.

Through a series of letters, this Caldecott Honor Book captures the spirit of a young gardener determined to fill her surroundings with flowers and to teach her uncle how to smile. It's a story that cleverly shows how writing letters keeps a family connected.

# The Reading & Writing Connection

Ask your students if they've ever seen a letter that was written long ago.

✳ Who wrote the letter?

✳ When was it written?

✳ Why do you think people save old letters?

✳ What do people learn from letters written long ago?

## AFTER-READING ACTIVITIES

# Write Away

Make a copy of the letter stationery on page 14 for each child, and have students try one of the following writing activities.

## Dear Lydia Grace

Lydia Grace writes letters to her family about the things she loves—flowers, gardens, and seeds. Have students write a letter to Lydia Grace telling her about something they loved in this story or something they love to do. Remind them to put the date at the top.

## Dear Uncle Jim

Once Lydia Grace goes home, she probably writes some letters to her Uncle Jim. Why not have students write one of those letters? Tell them to think of something Lydia Grace might say to her uncle or something she might ask.

_____

(date)

Dear _____ ,

_____

_____

_____

_____

_____

_____

_____

_____

P.S. _____

Scholastic Professional Books

# Write Ideas

## Personal Stationery

If Lydia Grace were making her own writing paper, she might put a few flowers at the top and the bottom, or even down the sides. Ask students what kind of writing paper they'd like to use. Have them design that stationery. Provide sheets of unlined paper and colored pencils for this project.

## A "News" Letter

Lydia Grace was away from home and sent letters to keep in touch with her family. Have students write a letter to an aunt, uncle, grandparent, or cousin that lives in another state. Ask children to share some news. Tell them to write about a school event or something newsworthy at home.

## An Indoor Garden

Lydia Grace filled the roof with flowers. Why not do the same in your classroom? On a bulletin board, post a colorful sign that reads: *Watch Our Garden Grow!* Display colored tissue paper, pipe cleaners, construction paper, and scraps of fabric. Encourage students to use these materials, along with lots of imagination, to design one-of-a-kind flowers. Have children plant each of their creations on the board. See how many colorful flowers it takes to fill this hands-on paper garden.

### Writing Tip

Remind students to write the date at the top of a letter to show the day the letter was written.

---

**ANOTHER GREAT MODEL FOR WRITING**

## Beethoven Lives Upstairs
by Barbara Nichol (Orchard, 1994)

Imagine having a famous person renting a room in your home. That's what happens to Christoph, a ten-year-old boy living in Vienna in 1822. Ludwig van Beethoven, the man who pounds on the piano all day and writes music on the walls, is now his upstairs neighbor.

Having recently lost his father, Christoph writes to an uncle studying music in Salzberg. The boy describes his embarrassing new boarder and asks Uncle Karl to convince Mother to force Beethoven out of the house.

Told through a series of letters, this book is perfect for older readers interested in writing letters, musical notes, and fan mail.

# Click, Clack, Moo: Cows That Type

by Doreen Cronin (Simon & Schuster, 2000)

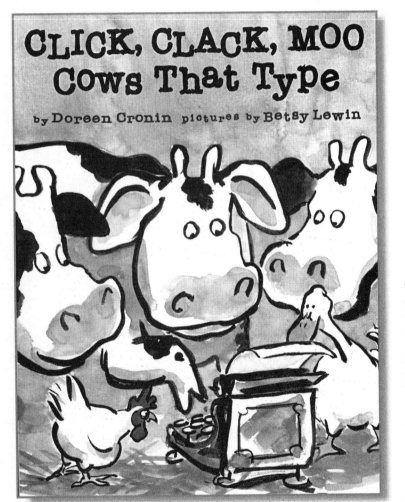

Farmer Brown hears the same sounds all day long. "Click, clack, moo! Clickety, clack, moo!" It seems his cows like to type. When those cows start leaving Dear Farmer Brown notes, the fun begins.

*Click, Clack, Moo: Cows That Type* is an award-winning story about a group of literate animals who discover the value of writing notes. Filled with clever notes, unusual requests, and funny salutations, this book is definitely a NOTEworthy read-aloud.

# The Reading & Writing Connection

Ask your students if they've ever typed on a typewriter.

❋ What sounds does a typewriter make?

❋ How many fingers do you use to type?

❋ Do you know anyone who uses a typewriter?

❋ How do you think a typewriter works?

## AFTER-READING ACTIVITIES

# Write Away

Make a copy of the note stationery on page 18 for each child, and have students try one of the following writing activities. Once students fold the note they might enjoy designing the front cover.

## Dear Farmer Brown

Farmer Brown's cows were writing him notes. Apparently, they had quite a few complaints. Have students write Farmer Brown another note from the cows. Ask them what else they think these funny animals might say. Remind children to have the cows sign the note.

## Dear Ducks

The ducks wrote Farmer Brown a funny note, too. It seems they weren't happy either! Ask students to write a note from Farmer Brown to the ducks. Have them imagine what the farmer might say. Remind children to have Farmer Brown sign the note.

A note for you...

Fold here - - - - - - - - - - - - - - - - - - - - - - - - - - - - - - - - - - - - - -

Dear _____ ,

_____

_____

_____

_____

                         _____

                         _____

Real-Life Writing Activities Based on Favorite Picture Books    Scholastic Professional Books

# Write Ideas

## A Note From a Pet

If cows can write notes, so can pets. Have students write a note from their own pet (or a pet they know.) Ask them to decide who that pet would write to. Then, tell them to imagine what that pet would say or what kind of complaint it might have. Remind children to have the pet sign the note.

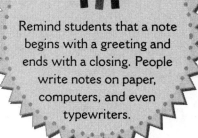

**Writing Tip**

Remind students that a note begins with a greeting and ends with a closing. People write notes on paper, computers, and even typewriters.

## Dear Author

Since Doreen Cronin, the author of *Click, Clack, Moo: Cows That Type*, collects antique typewriters, it's easy to imagine where she got the idea for her story. Have students write a short note to this author. Ask them to tell her what they liked most about her story. Remind children to sign their names.

## A Typewriting Center

Set up a manual or electric typewriter along with a stack of typing paper in a quiet corner. Post a colorful sign that reads: *Please type a note to a friend that describes how funny* Click, Clack, Moo: Cows That Type *is.* Invite students to visit the center to type a note and listen to the sounds of a typewriter.

---

**ANOTHER GREAT MODEL FOR WRITING**

## Mailing May
by Michael O. Tunnell (Greenwillow Books, 1997)

In 1914, traveling seventy-five miles to see your grandmother was almost impossible. A train ticket cost a full day's pay. So, May's parents had to think of another way to get their daughter across the Idaho mountains. The postal code didn't allow the mailing of lizards, insects, or anything smelly—but it didn't say anything about children. So . . . with fifty-three cents worth of stamps and a "Deliver to" label, this family would be *Mailing May*. Based on a true story, this book offers a glimpse of old stamps, mailbags, and mail cars. Plus, the author's note is the just-right prompt for writing notes to May.

# Lilly's Purple Plastic Purse

by Kevin Henkes (Greenwillow, 1996)

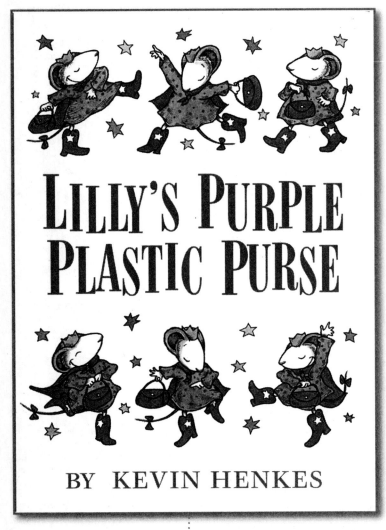

Lilly loves school, pointy pencils, squeaky chalk, and—most of all—her teacher, Mr. Slinger. But the day Lilly brings her new purple plastic purse, movie star glasses, and three jingling quarters to school, everything changes.

Since Lilly can't seem to wait for sharing time, Mr. Slinger is forced to take her purse away. So, Lilly sneaks an angry picture, complete with captions, into her favorite teacher's book bag. Imagine how Lilly feels later that day, when she finds the snack and thoughtful note that Mr. Slinger tucked inside her purse. Writing notes couldn't be more fun, thanks to Lilly and her purple plastic purse.

# The Reading & Writing Connection

Ask your students if they've ever written a note.

❋ When did you write it?

❋ Why did you write that note?

❋ When would a teacher write one?

❋ When do your family members write notes?

# Write Away

Make a copy of the note stationery on page 22 for each child, and have students try one of the following writing activities. Once students fold the note they might enjoy designing the front cover.

## A Note of Apology

Lilly and her purple plastic purse were disrupting Mr. Slinger's class. She owed her teacher an apology. Have students write a note of apology from Lilly to Mr. Slinger. Tell them to explain how sorry she was. Remind them to sign Lilly's name.

## Dear Mr. Slinger

Lilly's mother wrote Mr. Slinger a note apologizing for her daughter's behavior. At school, Lilly asked her teacher what that note said. Tell students to write a note of apology from Lilly's mother. Have them explain how sorry Lilly was. Remind them to sign the note from Lilly's mother.

# A Note for You...

Fold here -----------------------------------------------------------------

## Dear _____ ,

_____

_____

_____

_____

                                    _____

                                    _____

Real-Life Writing Activities Based on Favorite Picture Books    Scholastic Professional Books

# Write Ideas

## A *Lilly's Purple Plastic Purse* Pouch

Hang a purple paper pouch-like purse on a bulletin board. Above it, post a colorful sign that reads: *Please write a Dear Lilly note and drop it into the purse.* Just for fun, ask students to tell Lilly something they like about her, Mr. Slinger, or her story.

## A Love Note

Lilly loves school. She loves pointy pencils, squeaky chalk, and more. Why not have students write an "I Love School" note from Lilly to her teacher? Ask children to choose two or three things that Lilly might write about. Remind them to sign Lilly's name.

## A Lightbulb Lab

Lilly's classroom has a Lightbulb Lab, a place where students go to write, draw, and express their ideas. Plan to set up a Lightbulb Lab in a corner of your room. Stock the center with writing paper, pencils, drawing paper, and crayons, so children have a new place to go during their free time.

### Writing Tip

Remind students that a short note to say "I'm sorry" is called a note of apology.

# Lottie's New Beach Towel

by Petra Mathers (Atheneum Books for Young Readers, an Anne Schwartz Book, 1998)

Aunt Mattie's gift arrives just in time for Lottie's picnic with Herbie. The box contains a red and white polka-dotted beach towel along with a short note. Aunt Mattie writes that the towel might come in handy this summer. The fun begins when poor Lottie faces one beach problem after another and Aunt Mattie's thoughtful present saves the day.

Lottie's clever thank-you note at the end of this story is a perfect introduction to the art of writing thank-you notes.

# The Reading & Writing Connection

Ask your students if they like to receive presents.

✳ How do you thank a person for a gift?

✳ Do you usually write a note to say thank you?

✳ How do you let the person know how much you like the present?

✳ What else would you say about a gift?

**AFTER-READING ACTIVITIES**

# Write Away

Make a copy of the thank-you note stationery on page 26 for each child, and have students try one of the following writing activities. Have students fold the reproducible and write a note inside.

## A Thank-You Note From Lottie

At the end of the story, Lottie begins a thank-you note to her Aunt Mattie. Have students write a short note from Lottie to her aunt. Tell them to say thank you for the new beach towel. Remind children to sign Lottie's name.

## Thank You, Aunt Mattie

Suppose Aunt Mattie sent Lottie another gift that summer. Ask students to imagine a gift that would come in handy at the beach. Have them draw a sketch of that present. Then, tell children to write another thank-you note to Aunt Mattie. Remind them to sign Lottie's name.

Fold here

# Thank You

Real-Life Writing Activities Based on Favorite Picture Books    Scholastic Professional Books

# *Write Ideas*

## A Thank-You List

**H**ave students name some people that they would like to thank. Ask: *Did someone send you a gift? help you with homework? take you to a movie? teach you how to ride a bike?* Make a copy of the list stationery on page 58 or 62 for each child, and have students write the name of each person on their "Thank-You List." Remind children to order their list with the numerals 1, 2, 3, and so on.

## A Greeting Card

**S**ometimes people buy greeting cards that say thank you. The card may say thank you for a gift, for being a friend, for helping, or for being such a great coach. Have students think of one person to whom they would like to send a thank-you card. Have students design their own card. Provide markers, crayons, and colored pencils for the artwork and the message inside.

Writing
**Tip**

Encourage students to write thank-you notes for gifts received and to tell something they liked about the present.

# Officer Buckle and Gloria

by Peggy Rathmann (G. P. Putnam's Sons, 1995)

Officer Buckle is Napville's safety expert. He has safety tips tacked all over his bulletin board. But whenever he visits the local school to share his tips, no one seems to listen—until the day the new police dog named Gloria comes along. Without Officer Buckle knowing it, Gloria is acting out his safety tips and upstaging him. The next day when an envelope packed with thank-you notes arrives at the police station, every one of them has a drawing of Gloria on it. Buckle has no idea why.

This humorous Caldecott winner will make writing thank-you notes great fun. And it is sure to help readers appreciate the value of a note.

# The Reading & Writing Connection

Ask your students if they've ever had a guest speaker visit their classroom.

❋ Who came to visit?

❋ What did that person talk about?

❋ Did you learn something new from the guest speaker?

❋ How did you say thank you to that person?

# Write Away

Make a copy of the thank-you note stationery on page 26 or 30 for each child, and have students try one of the following writing activities. Have students fold the reproducible and write a note inside.

## Thank You, Officer Buckle and Gloria

Officer Buckle and Gloria visit schools to talk about safety. Have students pretend Officer Buckle and Gloria just visited your school. Tell them to write a thank-you note. Remind children to thank both visitors for coming.

## Thank You, Gloria

Officer Buckle might want to thank Gloria. Ask students to imagine what the police officer would say. Have children write that thank-you note from Officer Buckle. Remind them to sign Officer Buckle's name.

Fold here

Thank You

Real-Life Writing Activities Based on Favorite Picture Books    Scholastic Professional Books

# *Write Ideas*

## A Guest Speaker

Invite a local firefighter or police officer to visit the classroom to talk about fire safety or safety in the home. Schedule time for students to write little notes to say "thank you." Place all the notes into one large manila envelope and mail this packet to your guest speaker.

## Thank You, Dear Author

Have students write a thank-you note to Peggy Rathmann, the author of *Officer Buckle and Gloria*. Ask them to thank her for writing this award-winning book. Tell children to include something they like about the story or the characters. Remind them to sign their names.

## A Safety Tips List

Officer Buckle has more safety tips than anyone in Napville. See how many tips students can remember. Make a copy of the list stationery on page 58 or 62 for each child, and have students list the safety tips. Remind children to order their list with the numerals 1, 2, 3, and so on.

### Writing Tip

Have students write thank-you notes to people who speak at your school and to point out things they like about the talks.

---

**ANOTHER GREAT MODEL FOR WRITING**

# A Weekend With Wendell
by Kevin Henkes (William Morrow & Co., 1986)

When Wendell has to spend the weekend at Sophie's house, Sophie is not happy. Annoying Wendell finger-paints with peanut butter and jelly, leaves Sophie's crayons on the porch until they melt, and even tucks a "See you tomorrow" note under her pillow. All Sophie wants to know is, "When is Wendell going home?" This amusing houseguest story could be used to spark interest in writing notes, thank-you notes, house rules, and how-to's.

# A Letter to Amy

by Ezra Jack Keats (HarperCollins, 1968)

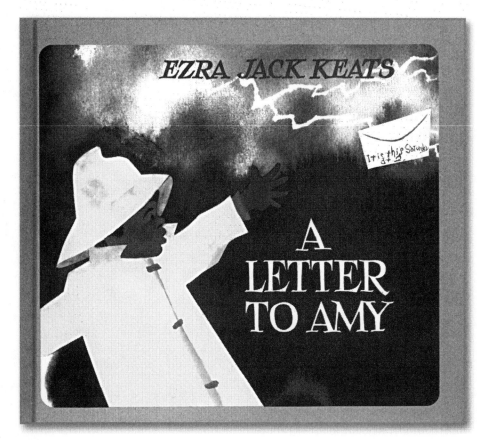

Peter's having a birthday party, but only one friend will receive a written invitation. Since Amy is the only girl being invited to an all-boy birthday party, Peter is determined to make her feel special.

With its simple text and trip-to-the-mailbox illustrations, *A Letter to Amy* is a delightful way to introduce the details of a written invitation. It's also a wonderful springboard for demonstrating how to address an envelope, mail a letter, and R.S.V.P.

# The Reading & Writing Connection

Ask your students if they make birthday party invitations or buy them.

❋ What kind of invitations do you like to make?

❋ What kind of invitations do you like to buy?

❋ How do you know what to write on each invitation?

❋ How do you decide which friends to invite?

# Write Away

Make a copy of the invitation stationery on page 34 for each child, and have students try the following writing activity. Once students fold the note they might enjoy designing the front cover.

## A Party Invitation

Peter wrote, "Please come to my birthday party," but forgot to tell when. So, he had to write it on the back of Amy's envelope. Ask students to write another invitation for Peter. Remind them to give all the party details.

Please Come to:

Given by:

Date:

Time:

Place:

R.S.V.P.:

34

Fold here

# Please Come to:

Given by: _____

Date: _____

Time: _____

Place: _____

R.S.V.P.: _____

Real-Life Writing Activities Based on Favorite Picture Books    Scholastic Professional Books

# *Write Ideas*

## An R.S.V.P.

Peter wasn't sure if Amy was coming to his party. He forgot to write the letters R.S.V.P. on the bottom of his invitation. *Répondez s'il vous plaît* (R.S.V.P.) means "please respond" in French. Ask students to pretend that those letters were on the invitation Peter sent. Amy would have to write a note to Peter, telling whether or not she could come to his party. Make a copy of the note stationery on page 18 or 22 for each child. Have students write that note from Amy to Peter.

## Address an Envelope

Peter printed his friend Amy's name and address on an envelope and then added a stamp. Have your students do the same. Using plain white envelopes with writing lines, tell then to write a friend's name on the first line and the friend's address on the next two lines. Ask children to design a colorful stamp to place in the corner, too.

## A Party Line

Peter invited his friends to come to his party. He probably called each boy on the phone. Set up a party-telephone line in your classroom. Use toy telephones or walkie-talkies. Ask students to choose partners and role-play calling a friend to invite him or her to a party. Have the rest of the class listen in on each phone conversation.

**Writing Tip**

Remind students that it's fun to send party invitations. People write everything from fancy notes to birthday poems and Please Come cards.

# Miss Spider's Tea Party

by David Kirk (Scholastic Press, 1994)

No one wants to come to Miss Spider's tea party, even though she's extending personal invitations. It seems that all the other insects are afraid of being eaten. But thanks to one small wet moth and Miss Spider's wonderful hospitality, this charming arachnid finally gets to host a tea party for twelve.

This rhyming counting book will stir up some interesting how-to discussions about the art of reading, writing, and receiving invitations.

# The Reading & Writing Connection

Ask your students if they've ever been invited to a tea party.

✳ Who invited you?

✳ What kind of invitation did you receive?

✳ What was served at the tea party?

✳ Who else came to the party?

# Write Away

Make a copy of the invitation stationery on page 38 for each child, and have students try one of the following writing activities. Remind them to include the specifics of who, what, where, and when. Once students fold the note they might enjoy designing the front cover.

## An Invitation to Tea

Miss Spider asked her fellow bugs to tea. What if she handed out tea party invitations instead? Ask students to decide what her invitation would say. Have them write that invitation for Miss Spider.

## A Party Invitation

Suppose Miss Spider decides to have another party. Will it be a birthday party, a costume party, or a surprise party? Ask students to decide. Then, have students write the invitation for Miss Spider.

Please Come to:

Given by: .................

Date: .................

Time: .................

Place: .................

R.S.V.P.: .................

38

37

Fold here

# Please Come to:

Given by: _____

Date: _____

Time: _____

Place: _____

R.S.V.P.: _____

Real-Life Writing Activities Based on Favorite Picture Books    Scholastic Professional Books

# Write Ideas

## A Web Sight

On a bulletin board, use white string and tacks to create a spider web. Have students picture the kind of tea party invitation Miss Spider might make and send. Ask children to design that invitation. Remind them to tell who, what, where, and when. Then, post these colorful tea party invitations all over your Web Sight.

## An Author's Tea

Choose one or two of the class's favorite authors to share with parents. Plan a simple tea party with a menu of sun tea (a hands-on science lesson) and cookies. Before the big event, have each child design an original tea party invitation to take home. Remind students that these invitations should tell who is giving the party, what kind of party it is, and where and when the party will take place.

The morning of the event, have children place four tea bags in a lidded two-quart container of cold water. Set the container on a windowsill or in direct sunlight for two to three hours, or until desired strength. Remove the tea bags and have students serve the tea over ice.

## A Guest List

Miss Spider invited two beetles, three fireflies, four bumblebees, and more to her tea party. Make a copy of the list stationery on page 58 or 62 for each child. Ask students to duplicate Miss Spider's guest list. Have them list all the bugs invited to tea with Miss Spider.

### Writing Tip

Remind students that party invitations need to answer these questions: *Who is giving the party? What kind of party is it? When is the party? Where is the party?*

---

**ANOTHER GREAT MODEL FOR WRITING**

## The Secret Birthday Message
by Eric Carle (HarperCollins, 1972)

Imagine finding a secret birthday message tucked underneath your pillow. In this story, Tim finds a rebus letter with specific directions to follow. From the birthday letter to the die-cut holes and the page-turning illustrations, this book shows how easy it is to write simple directions and secret messages.

# Where Do Balloons Go? An Uplifting Mystery

by Jamie Lee Curtis (Joanna Cotler Books, HarperCollins, 2000)

Where do balloons go? Does anyone know? It's definitely a mystery. But consider the possibilities.

Jamie Lee Curtis's rhyming text raises questions every child will appreciate. While taking readers to different parts of the world, this delightful adventure even asks whether balloons ever write postcards, e-mail, and faxes. And the last two pages of this book, filled with colorful postcards, are guaranteed to spark some interest in collecting, writing, and sending postcards.

# The Reading & Writing Connection

Ask your students if they've ever lost a balloon.

✳ How did you feel when you saw your balloon floating away?

✳ Where do you think your balloon was going?

✳ Have you ever seen a postcard with pictures of balloons on it?

✳ What other kinds of postcards have you seen?

## AFTER-READING ACTIVITIES

# Write Away

Make a copy of the postcard stationery on page 42 for each child, and have students try one of the following writing activities. Invite students to draw a picture on the front of the postcard, and then use words to describe it in the picture-description box.

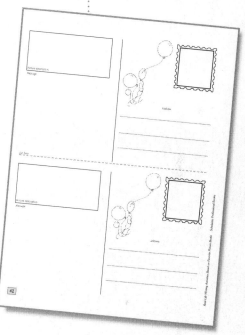

## A Postcard From Far Away

Invite children to think about a time when they lost a balloon. Ask: *What if that balloon sent you a postcard? From which faraway place do you think the balloon would send mail? What do you think the postcard would say? How would it be signed?* Have students write that postcard.

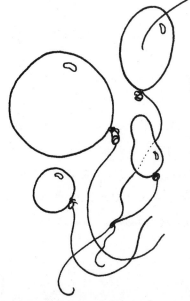

## A Postcard From Balloonville

Have students pretend they are taking an imaginary trip to a place called Balloonville. Ask them to picture what that place looks like and think about what they would do there. Tell them to write a postcard to a friend about the trip to Balloonville.

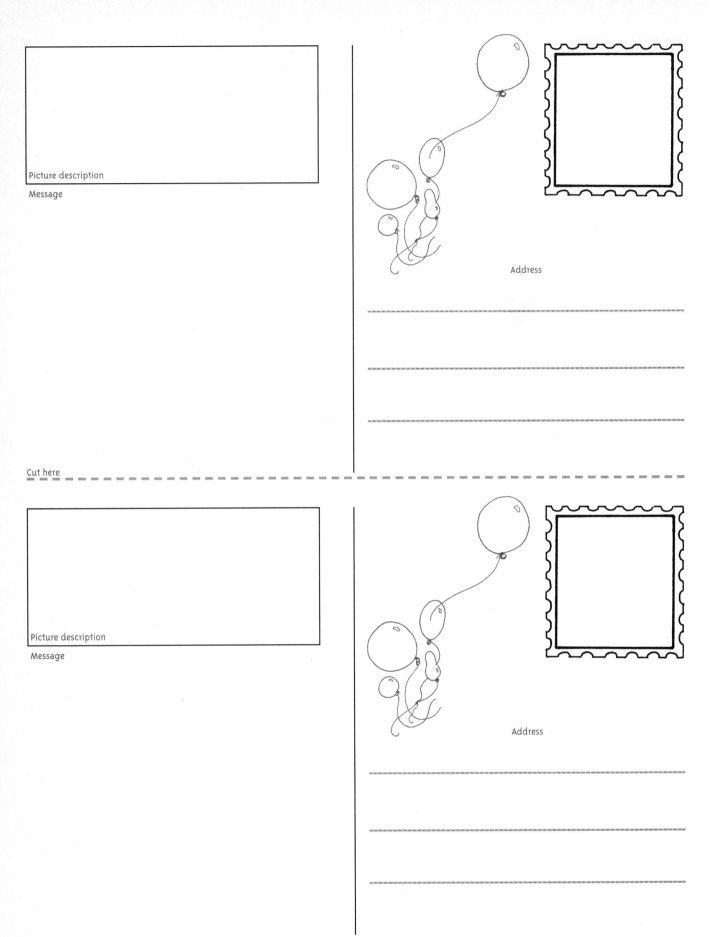

Picture description

Message

Address

Cut here

Picture description

Message

Address

42

# Write Ideas

## Message Balloons

In the story *Where Do Balloons Go?* the author wonders if plain balloons know how to read balloons printed with words. Ask if students have ever seen a balloon that said "Happy Birthday," "Get Well," or "Congratulations." Tell children to think of another message that could be printed on a balloon. On large paper balloons, have them write a few words and add some decorations. Attach pieces of string and display these creations around the classroom.

**Writing Tip**

Encourage students to send a postcard to a friend or relative. All they need to do is choose a postcard, write a brief note, include an address and stamp, and mail it.

## A Balloon Launch

All you need for a balloon launch is a package of balloons, a tank of helium, a ball of string, and blank name tags. Have each student print his or her name and your town and state information on the tags. Attach one tag to the string of each inflated balloon. Gather the students on the playground. At the count of three, tell children to let go of the balloons and watch them disappear. (You can also have students make colorful invitations to send to family members before the launch or have them write about the experience in a diary or a journal entry.)

## A Lost Balloon Poster

Have students pretend they just lost a brand-new balloon. Ask: *What color is it? Which direction did it go in?* Tell them to make a Missing Balloon sign to hang in the neighborhood. Remind children to write their names and phone numbers on the poster.

## A How-To

Have students explain how to blow up a balloon. Ask them to think about what to do first, next, and last. Make a copy of the how-to stationery on page 66 or 70 for each child and have students write step-by-step instructions.

# Stringbean's Trip to the Shining Sea

by Vera B. Williams and Jennifer Williams (William Morrow & Company, 1988)

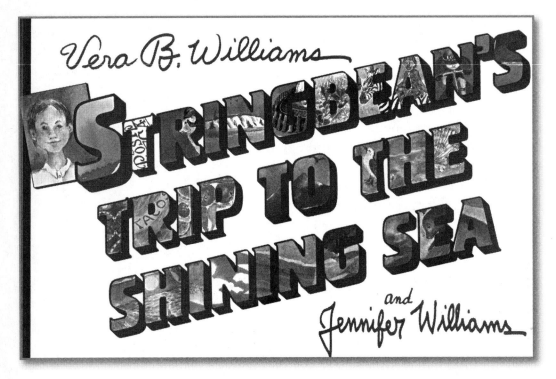

One summer, Stringbean Coe and his big brother Fred took a cross-country trip in Fred's truck. Through a series of postcards, the younger boy kept in touch with his parents and grandfather. Stringbean shares details with his family as he tells the story of that long, memorable trip.

This award-winning book, packed with colorful postcards, captioned snapshots, and interesting landmarks, is a travel story guaranteed to make reading, writing, and sending postcards more fun.

# The Reading & Writing Connection

Ask your students if they've ever received a postcard.

❋ Who sent you a postcard?

❋ From where was it sent?

❋ Have you ever sent someone a postcard?

❋ If so, what kind of postcard did you send?

# Write Away

Make a copy of the postcard stationery on page 46 for each child, and have students try one of the following writing activities. Invite students to draw a picture on the front of the postcard, and then use words to describe it in the picture-description box.

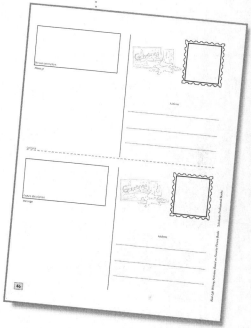

## A Postcard From Stringbean

As he travels cross-country, Stringbean writes postcards describing the different places he sees. Have students pretend that along the way, Stringbean visits their town or city. Ask them to imagine what Stringbean would say about his visit. Tell children to write that postcard for him. Remind them to sign Stringbean's name.

## A Postcard to Stringbean

Everyone has a favorite place. Ask students to write a postcard from theirs. Suggest that they draw a picture. Then, have them write to Stringbean to tell him why the favorite place is so special. Remind children to sign their names.

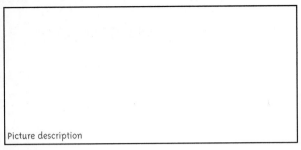

Picture description

Message

Address

_____

_____

_____

Cut here

Picture description

Message

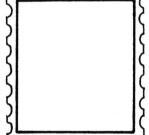

Address

_____

_____

_____

Real-Life Writing Activities Based on Favorite Picture Books    Scholastic Professional Books

## Write Ideas

### A Picture Postcard

Show students how to take a cross-country trip without leaving the classroom. Set up a picture postcard bulletin board display. Ask students to bring in postcards from the South, the West, the Rockies, Washington, D.C., national parks, and other places in the United States. Post each card, picture side showing. Have children write brief captions for each card they contribute. Use this travel exhibit to get them even more excited about traveling to different parts of the country.

### A Postcard Contest

Plan a design-a-postcard contest. Post specific guidelines on a classroom message board. Invite every student to enter. Here are some contest guidelines to get you started:

#### Contest Rules
Only one entry per student.
The postcard must show a place somewhere in the United States.
All postcards must be created on a 9- by 12-inch sheet of oak tag.
Contestants may use crayons, markers, colored pencils, or magazine cutouts.
All postcards must be received before Thursday at 3:00 P.M.

### Address a Postcard

Have students send a postcard to a friend or relative. Show them where to write the name and address. Remind them to include the zip code. Then, as a class, take a walk to the nearest mailbox and mail them. (Don't forget to add stamps!)

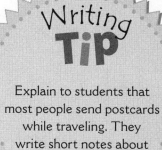

Writing **Tip**

Explain to students that most people send postcards while traveling. They write short notes about places they see.

---

ANOTHER GREAT MODEL FOR WRITING

## Three Days on a River in a Red Canoe
by Vera B. Williams (Greenwillow, 1981)

This camping trip begins with a For Sale sign posted on a neighbor's front lawn and the purchase of a used red canoe. Two moms and two children pool their money to get ready for this three-day adventure. From mapping out the trip, to planning a shopping list, pitching a tent, and cooking over a campfire, this book is filled with interesting details. It's a terrific read-aloud for writing lists, easy-to-prepare recipes, and how-to's.

# Flip's Fantastic Journal

by Angelo DeCesare (Dutton Children's Books, 1999)

Flip likes to draw and play but he doesn't like to write. So when his teacher, Ms. Flea-Collar, insists that he keep a journal and write in it every day, even on Saturdays and Sundays, the poor little fellow is not happy.

This hand-printed notebook story begins with clever black-and-white pencil sketches and ends with imaginative drawings colored with markers. With its authentic journal entries and childlike charm, *Flip's Fantastic Journal* will spark lots of interest in keeping a daily journal. Plus, even beginning writers will like the idea of using their imaginations to write about what might have happened.

# The Reading & Writing Connection

Ask your students if they've ever known anyone who keeps a journal.

❊ What kinds of things do you think people write about in a journal?

❊ What would you write about if you kept a journal?

❊ Do you think you'd like to write in a journal every day?
Why or why not?

❊ How would you feel if your teacher said you had to?

# Write Away

Make a copy of the journal stationery on page 50 for each child, and have students try one of the following writing activities. Remind them to draw stick figures, too.

## A V.I.P. Page

In his journal, Flip introduces readers to his mom, his sister, Sniffie, and his best friend, Muzz. Have students introduce you to the very important people in their lives—moms, dads, brothers, sisters, best friends, and so on. Ask them to write a journal page just like Flip's.

## A Saturday Page

In his journal, Flip writes about Saturday. He says nothing happened. Have students write about what they did last Saturday. Tell them to write about where they went, what they played, or what they saw.

## A Make-Things-Up Page

When Ms. Flea-Collar says it's okay to make things up, finally Flip gets excited about journal writing. Ask students to make things up. Tell them to write about something that never really happened.

TOP SECRET!!!

No Peeking!

PRIVATE!!

_____
(date)

Real-Life Writing Activities Based on Favorite Picture Books    Scholastic Professional Books

# Write Ideas

## A Message from Ms. Flea-Collar

In a corner of the classroom, post this colorful reminder from Ms. Flea-Collar: *Write in your journal every day! Don't forget Saturday and Sunday. You can tell what really happens or you can make things up.* First thing each morning, schedule some writing time for students.

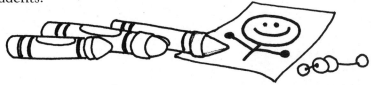

## Funny Pages

Make seven copies of the journal stationery on page 50 or 54 for each child, and ask students to keep a journal for one week. Have them write about a funny thing that happens each day. At the end of the week, suggest that children reread their journals and decide which of his or her descriptions is the funniest. Tell them to share that piece of writing with a friend or classmate.

## Word Play

Have students make a list of words and phrases that describe themselves. Ask: *Are you a basketball player? a student? a brother? a son? Are you shy? friendly? talkative? bossy? Do you like to draw? ride bikes? read? play the piano?* Tell children to see how many things they can think of. Then, encourage them to use this list to write about themselves and to try to fill one whole page in their journals.

### Writing Tip

Remind students that it's fun to keep journals. They're great to write in every day to record what really happens or what you imagine could happen.

# Birdie's Lighthouse

by Deborah Hopkinson (Atheneum Books for Young Readers,
an Anne Schwartz Book, 1997)

Once Birdie's family moves to Turtle Island, a tiny island off the coast of Maine, her only friend is her diary. So, the diary is where the ten-year-old writes about her parents, her brother and sister, the weather, the sea, and the interesting things her father, the lighthouse keeper, teaches her. When her father becomes ill, there's no one but Birdie to take charge of the lighthouse.

Told in diary form, *Birdie's Lighthouse* shares the day-to-day observations of a young girl whose life centers on the lighthouse. Set in the mid-1800s, it's a story that makes it easy to see the value of keeping a diary or logbook.

# The Reading & Writing Connection

Ask your students if they've ever written in a diary.

✽ Did that diary have a lock and key?

✽ Why do you think diaries have a lock and key?

✽ What do people usually write about in their diaries?

✽ What would you write about in a diary?

# Write Away

Make a copy of the journal stationery on page 54 for each child, and have students try one of the following writing activities. Remind children to put the date at the top of the page.

## A Diary Page

In her diary, Birdie writes about helping her father at the lighthouse. Ask students to imagine spending a day with a lighthouse keeper. Have them write a description of what they see, what they do, or what they learn.

## A Weather Page

In her diary, Birdie writes about the weather. Have students write a diary page describing today's weather. Tell them to choose their words carefully.

## A Favorite Place Page

In her diary, Birdie writes about the sea and the lighthouse, her favorite places. Ask students to write a diary page describing their favorite place.

_____
(date)

# Dear Diary,

_____

_____

_____

_____

_____

_____

_____

_____

Real-Life Writing Activities Based on Favorite Picture Books    Scholastic Professional Books

# Write Ideas

## A Seven-Day Diary

**S**how students how to make their own diaries. Have them fold a large piece of colored paper in half, place seven sheets of writing paper inside, and staple the booklet together. Suggest that they use crayons to decorate the front cover. Ask children to write in these diaries every day for one week. Tell them to write about their thoughts, observations, or feelings. Remind them to begin each page with the date.

## A Log

**A** logbook is a place to write observations. Sea captains and lighthouse keepers keep logs. In this story, both the lighthouse keeper and his daughter, Birdie, wrote in the logbook. Ask students to try writing in a logbook. Pass out blank logbook pages with writing lines. Then have them imagine they're in a lighthouse. Say: *Look around you. Do you see any ships approaching? Is there a storm coming?* Suggest that students write what they imagine. Remind them to include the date and to sign their names.

## An Author's Note

**R**ead aloud the Author's Note on the last page of *Birdie's Lighthouse*. The writer explains that even though Birdie Holland is not a real person, her story was inspired by a number of lighthouse heroines. Make a copy of the letter stationery on page 10 or 14 for each child, and have students write a note to Deborah Hopkinson, the author of *Birdie's Lighthouse*. Ask them to tell her about a favorite hero or heroine. Remind children to sign their names.

### Writing Tip

Encourage students to write about their thoughts, feelings, or observations in a diary. Tell them to be sure to put the date at the top of each diary entry.

---

**ANOTHER GREAT MODEL FOR WRITING**

# Emily's First 100 Days of School
by Rosemary Wells (Hyperion, 2000)

**T**his book begins with an author's note and ends with a charming letter from Emily to her mother and father. It's a fitting read-aloud for young readers getting ready to write notes and letters. The fact that Emily has a notebook, keeps a math journal, and is very busy learning should spark some interest in numbers and journal writing.

# Wemberly Worried

by Kevin Henkes (Greenwillow, 2000)

Wemberly is a worrier. The poor mouse worries about big things, little things, and everything in between. When the time comes for Wemberly to start school, her list of worries grows even longer.

From Wemberly's birthday to her first day at school, this book offers delightful ways to focus on the value of making guest lists, back-to-school lists, and even worry lists.

# The Reading & Writing Connection

Ask your students if they've ever worried.

✳ What do you worry about?

✳ What does your friend worry about?

✳ Do you think most kids worry about the same kinds of things?

✳ Have you ever jotted down some of the things that worry you?

# Write Away

Make a copy of the list stationery on page 58 or 62 for each child and cut apart. Have students use one list for each of the following writing activities. Remind children to order their list with the numerals 1, 2, 3, 4, and 5.

## Wemberly's Worry List

Wemberly worries about everything. Ask students to list five things this mouse worries about.

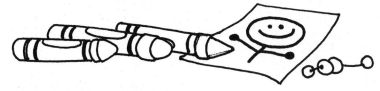

## Top-Five Worries List

No one worries as much as Wemberly does! But students probably share many of the same concerns. Have them make a list of the five things that worry them most.

# My List

# My List

Cut here

Real-Life Writing Activities Based on Favorite Picture Books    Scholastic Professional Books

# *Write Ideas*

## Guest List

Wemberly worries that no one will come to her birthday party. Ask students to give some thought to their own birthday parties. Have them make a guest list of five people they would invite.

## Back-to-School List

Wemberly worries about the first day of school. Ask students to think about getting ready for school each year. Tell them to make a list of five school supplies they need to buy.

## T-Shirt Message

Wemberly's grandmother wears a T-shirt that says "Go With the Flow." She also points to a wall hanging that reads "Take It as It Comes." Have students imagine what kind of T-shirt Wemberly would wear. Make a copy of the T-shirt pattern on page 82 for each child. Tell students to design that shirt with just the right message.

Writing
Tip

Ask students to make five-item lists of things they want to remember, need to buy, or have to do.

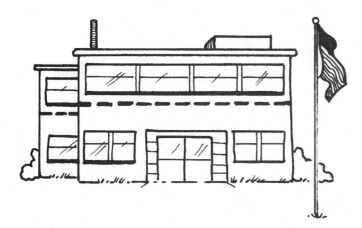

# Olivia

By Ian Falconer (Atheneum Books for Young Readers,
an Anne Schwartz Book, 2000)

Olivia seems to know how to wear everyone out, including herself. Before deciding what to wear, she has to try on everything. At naptime, she's never really sleepy. And even when it's time for bed, Olivia wants to read five books rather than just one.

In this Caldecott Honor Book, a delightful pig shows how much fun a trip to the beach and the art museum can be. With her boundless energy and her charming personality, Olivia is guaranteed to get students excited about writing lists.

# The Reading & Writing Connection

Ask your students what they will do after school today.

✳ What will you do after school tomorrow?

✳ Do you ever get tired from all your after-school activities?

✳ How does your family keep track of all your activities?

✳ How do you remember all the things you have to do?

## AFTER-READING ACTIVITIES

# Write Away

Make a copy of the list stationery on page 58 or 62 for each child and cut apart. Have students use one list for each of the following writing activities. Remind children to order their list with the numerals 1, 2, 3, 4, and 5.

## What-Olivia-Likes-to-Do List

Olivia likes to do so many things. Have students make a list of five things this pig does for fun.

## What-I-Like-to-Do List

Everyone has things they like to do. Have students make a list of five of their favorite activities.

## A Going-to-the-Beach List

Olivia always takes things to the beach. Have students make a list of five things they like to take to the beach.

## My Favorite Places

Olivia likes to go to the beach and the art museum. She doesn't like to go to bed. Have students make a list of five places they like to go.

## My Favorite Books

Olivia wants to read five books before bed. Have students make a list of five books they love to read.

## A Word List

Olivia is a very funny character. Have students make a list of five words that describe her.

# My List

# My List

# *Write Ideas*

## Arts and Letters

Olivia loves going to the art museum to look at her favorite painting by Degas. And she gets into trouble when she paints a "Jackson Pollock" on her bedroom wall. Have students show the kind of artwork they enjoy most. Tell them to design their own stationery. Hand out two or three sheets of unlined writing paper and colored pencils. Ask them to add a colorful border, a small drawing, a pattern, or fancy initials to each page.

## A How-To

Olivia is good at singing, dancing, dressing up, painting on walls, and building sand castles. Ask students to think of something they're good at. Suggest they share what they know. Make a copy of the how-to stationery on page 66 or 70 for each child. Have students write a how-to that explains how to make something or do something.

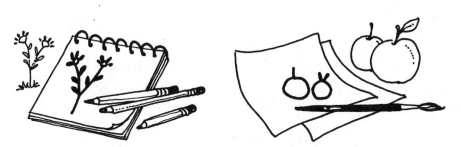

**Writing Tip**

Remind students that writing lists is a helpful way to jot down and recall important words or phrases.

---

### ANOTHER GREAT MODEL FOR WRITING

## Max Found Two Sticks

by Brian Pinkney (Simon & Schuster Books for Young Readers, 1994)

Max finds two sticks and takes us on a musical adventure. Using Grandpa's cleaning bucket, some discarded hatboxes, empty soda bottles, and more, the young boy shows readers how easy it is to make music. This book is perfect for drumming up some interest in writing how-to's and making lists.

# Joseph Had a Little Overcoat

by Simms Taback (Viking, 1999)

Joseph had a little overcoat that was full of holes, and so is this delightful Caldecott winner. With its simple text and die-cut openings, readers take a peek at how one man cleverly turns his shabby overcoat into a jacket, vest, scarf, and necktie, and then, much more.

*Joseph Had a Little Overcoat* illustrates the importance of following a step-by-step process and sequencing. It's a delightful introduction for writing how-to's.

# The Reading & Writing Connection

Ask your students if they've ever made something out of old newspapers.

✳ What did you make? How did you make it?

✳ Have you ever made something out of an empty box?
   If so, what did you make?

✳ Did someone ever show you how to twist a balloon into an animal?

✳ What else did someone show you how to make?

# Write Away

Make a copy of the how-to stationery on page 66 for each child, and have students try one of the following writing activities. Remind them to give step-by-step instructions and draw pictures in the boxes.

## A Makeover

Joseph turned an overcoat into a jacket, a jacket into a vest, and a vest into a scarf. Have students choose their favorite makeover from the story. Tell them to write a how-to explaining how to turn one thing into another.

## How to Make a Book

Joseph started with a little overcoat and ended up making a very special book. Have students write a how-to about how they would make a book.

## How to Teach a Song

Joseph's favorite song is "I Had a Little Overcoat." Have students write about how they would teach this song to a friend.

# How to:

........................................................................................................................

1. _____

   _____

   _____

2. _____

   _____

   _____

3. _____

   _____

   _____

4. _____

   _____

   _____

Real-Life Writing Activities Based on Favorite Picture Books    Scholastic Professional Books

# Write Ideas

## A Get-Well Note

Remember when Joseph was sick in bed. He needed a pot of tea and his little handkerchief. Make a copy of the note stationery on page 18 or 22 for each child. Have students write a get-well note to Joseph. Ask them to write something to make him feel better. Remind children to sign their names.

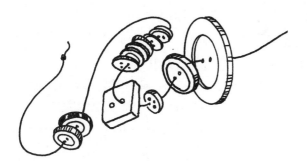

**Writing Tip**

Remind students that a how-to explains how to make something step-by-step.

## Little Overcoat Buttons

Joseph created a special button and so can everyone in your class. Have students cut out paper circles and turn them into *Joseph Had a Little Overcoat* song buttons. On the chalkboard, post easy-to-read instructions. Tell children to follow them step by step. Then, invite everyone to show off his or her new buttons as you sing "I Had a Little Overcoat" together.

## A Makeover Party

Gather old newspapers, magazines, empty paper-towel rolls, empty boxes, and other items. Display these items in an art center. Make time for children to look over the objects and think about possibilities. Have them choose one item and do what Joseph did—turn that something into something else! Tell children to use their imaginations, plus scissors, paste, and crayons to see what they can create.

# Drawing Lessons From a Bear

by David McPhail (Little, Brown & Company, 2000)

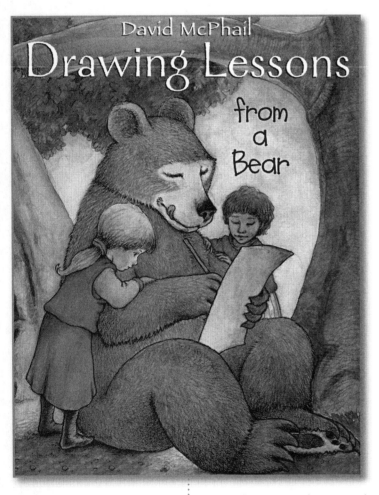

Thanks to his mother, a young bear gets how-to-be-a-bear lessons. She shows him how to walk, sit, find berries, catch fish, and climb trees. When that same little bear begins making claw marks all over their den floor, he realizes how much he loves to draw. From searching for scraps of paper, to copying pictures in the museum, to waking up in winter just to draw—this talented little bear makes learning how to be an artist great fun.

*Drawing Lessons From a Bear* will delight readers who are wondering how to become artists, musicians, dancers, or ball players. Plus, inside the front and back covers of this book are David McPhail's pencil sketches along with his wonderful how-to tips for beginning artists.

# The Reading & Writing Connection

Ask your students if a family member ever taught them how to do something.

✳ What did that person teach you how to do?

✳ Did they show you how or did they tell you how?

✳ Did you ever teach someone how to do something?

✳ What did you teach them how to do?

# Write Away

Make a copy of the how-to stationery on page 70 for each child, and have students try one of the following writing activities. Tell children to write at least three helpful tips using action verbs and draw pictures in the boxes.

## An Animal How-to

In this story, a mother bear shows her son how to stand, sit, and walk. She teaches him how to be a bear. Have students write a simple how-to. Ask them to explain how to be a bear, elephant, lion, mouse, or any animal they choose.

## A How-to

The little bear learned how to be an artist. Have students choose something they'd like to be and write a simple how-to. Ask them to explain how to be an artist, writer, ballplayer, dancer, magician, or anything else they'd like to be.

# How to:

_____

1. _____

   _____

   _____

2. _____

   _____

   _____

3. _____

   _____

   _____

4. _____

   _____

   _____

Real-Life Writing Activities Based on Favorite Picture Books   Scholastic Professional Books

# Write Ideas

## Drawing Lessons

Ask students to explain how to make a picture of an animal, house, boat, or anything else they like to draw. First, have them draw the picture. To simplify things, suggest they only use basic shapes—circles, squares, rectangles, and triangles. Then, tell them to write step-by-step instructions.

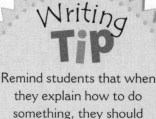

**Writing Tip**

Remind students that when they explain how to do something, they should use action verbs.

## An Artist's Studio

As an ongoing project, fill a box with fabric remnants, pieces of wrapping paper, string, ribbon, foil, and other materials. Place drawing paper, paste, colored pencils, and markers on a table. Have students use the space as a hands-on art center, a place for young artists to experiment and share ideas.

## An Artist's List

Artists work with all different kinds of materials. Invite students to think of five art supplies they'd like to buy. Make a copy of the list stationery on page 58 or 62 for each child. Ask students to make a list. Remind children to order their list with the numerals 1, 2, 3, 4, and 5.

---

**ANOTHER GREAT MODEL FOR WRITING**

## Dear Juno
by Soyung Pak (Viking, 1999)

When Juno receives a letter from his grandmother in Korea, he can't wait to open it. Even though he can't read the letter without his parents' help, the boy slits the envelope. Tucked inside, he finds a photo and a dried flower. And that's how Juno figures out what the Korean words in his grandma's letter mean. *Dear Juno*, about a letter written in a foreign language, could be used to spark interest in writing to pen pals or distant relatives.

# Pumpkin Soup

by Helen Cooper (Farrar, Straus & Giroux, 1999)

Cat, Squirrel, and Duck always make the most delicious pumpkin soup together. Cat slices the pumpkin, Squirrel stirs in the water, and Duck adds just the right amount of salt. But one day, Duck decides that he wants to be the one to stir the soup. That's when the trouble begins and one very angry Duck packs his belongings and waddles away from home.

The secret to making great pumpkin soup should stir up some interesting discussions about food, cooking, and following recipes. This charming story, with its author's note and real pumpkin soup recipe at the end, will add just the right flavor to your recipe-writing activities.

# The Reading & Writing Connection

Ask your students if they've ever helped make soup.

✳ What kind of soup did you make?

✳ What ingredients did you use?

✳ What did you do to help?

✳ How did you know what to do?

# Write Away

Make a copy of the recipe stationery on page 74 for each child, and have students try one of the following writing activities. Tell them to write simple instructions.

## A Pumpkin Soup Recipe

Cat, Squirrel, and Duck make the best pumpkin soup. Ask students to jot down that special recipe. Have students list the three main ingredients. Remind children to explain what happens first, next, and last.

## A Pumpkin Seed Recipe

Cat, Squirrel, and Duck could make a fun snack using pumpkin seeds. All they have to do is scoop out the seeds, wash and dry them, then toast them with a little oil and salt. Ask students to write their own recipe and title it "Toasted Pumpkin Seeds." Have them list the three main ingredients.

# A Recipe for:

## What you will need:

_____     _____

_____     _____

_____     _____

## How to make this dish!

_____

_____

_____

_____

_____

## From the Kitchen of:

_____

(name)

Real-Life Writing Activities Based on Favorite Picture Books    Scholastic Professional Books

# Write Ideas

## A Soup Label

What if Cat, Squirrel, and Duck decided to sell their famous pumpkin soup? They'd need a catchy name and a colorful label for the soup can. Ask students to name the soup and design the can. Tell them to print the name of the soup on the can and to decorate the label. Remind them to write simple "warm and serve" directions, too.

## A SOUPer Bowl Display

Cut colored paper to make a giant bowl for pumpkin soup that looks just like the bowl Cat, Squirrel, and Duck use. Attach the soup bowl to the center of a bulletin board. Stack the student-designed pumpkin soup cans from the previous activity around the bowl.

## A Pumpkin How-To

Pumpkin soup makes us think of autumn. Have students describe something else they know how to make with pumpkins. Ask them to explain how to paint a pumpkin face, carve a jack-o-lantern, cut out a paper pumpkin, or make a pumpkin treat. Make a copy of the how-to stationery on page 66 or 70 for each child. Tell students to write their own how-to instructions.

Writing Tip

Explain to students that a recipe lists the needed ingredients. It also tells what to do first, next, and last.

# Cook-a-Doodle-Doo!

by Janet Stevens and Susan Stevens Crummel
(Harcourt Brace and Company, 1999)

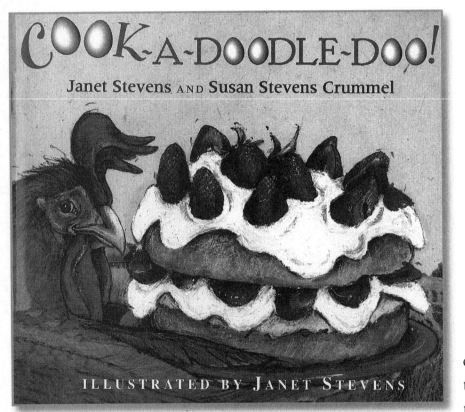

Rooster is sick of chicken feed. So, he decides to try cooking for the very first time. While skimming through the Little Red Hen's cookbook, *The Joy of Cooking Alone*, Rooster discovers that his well-known great-grandmother didn't just bake bread. With his helpers Turtle, Iguana, and Pig, Rooster follows his great-grandmother's Magnificent Strawberry Shortcake recipe and the fun in the kitchen begins.

This humorous tale, along with the factual information all along the margins, will appeal to cooks of all ages. It's a read-aloud guaranteed to give children a taste of reading, writing, and making recipes.

# The Reading & Writing Connection

Ask your students if they've ever baked a cake.

✱ What kind of cake did you make?

✱ Which ingredients did you use?

✱ What did you do to help?

✱ How did you know what to do?

# Write Away

Make a copy of the recipe stationery on page 78 for each child, and have students try one of the following writing activities. Remind them to explain what to do first, next, and last.

## A Strawberry Shortcake Recipe

Rooster baked the cake, whipped the cream, and washed the strawberries. Now, he's ready to put together his Strawberry Shortcake. Have students write a step-by-step recipe for Rooster.

## A Mud Pie Recipe

There might be some silly misunderstandings if Rooster, Turtle, Iguana, and Pig decide to make a Mud Pie. Have students name three ingredients they might use. Ask them to write a recipe for Mud Pie.

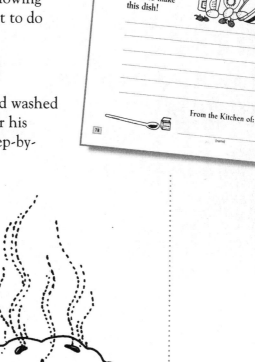

# A Recipe for:

## What you will need:

_____     _____

_____     _____

_____     _____

## How to make this dish!

_____

_____

_____

_____

_____

## From the Kitchen of:

_____
(name)

Real-Life Writing Activities Based on Favorite Picture Books    Scholastic Professional Books

## Write Ideas

### A Class Cookbook

Have students vote to decide whether to share favorite family recipes, special holiday recipes, or simple no-cook recipes. Then ask each student to write an easy-to-read recipe page for a booklet titled *The Joy of Cooking Together*. Make photocopies of each student's recipe, one for each child. Tell students to assemble the class's recipes inside a colorful folder.

### Cooks Corner

Set up a cooking center stocked with rolling pins, aprons, plastic measuring cups, measuring spoons, and other cooking tools. Include pencils and a set of lined index cards. Invite students to visit the center and create imaginary foods. Ask them to write recipe cards to record their delicious creations.

### A Strawberry Surprise

Strawberries can be used in all kinds of dishes. Ask students to think of something they'd make with strawberries. Tell them to list the ingredients. Then have them write an easy-to-read recipe.

**Writing Tip**

Remind students that a recipe is a set of step-by-step instructions. It explains how to make or cook food.

---

**ANOTHER GREAT MODEL FOR WRITING**

## Aloha, Dolores

by Barbara Samuels (Dorling Kindersley, 2000)

Convinced she's going to win the Meow Munchies cat food contest, Dolores is already planning her trip to Hawaii. All she has to do is finish the sentence on the pet food box, include a photo of her cat, Duncan, and collect three Meow Munchies box tops. From entering contests to following contest rules and finishing advertising slogans, Dolores will definitely make writing how-to's, messages, and step-by-step instructions more fun.

# Clarice Bean: That's Me

by Lauren Child (Candlewick Press, 1999)

All Clarice Bean wants is a little peace and quiet, but this young girl has to share a room with her annoying little brother, Minal Cricket. Plus, she has to deal with a big brother who wears a "Shut Up and Go Away" T-shirt and hangs a "No Entry" sign on his bedroom door. As Clarice introduces readers to her teenage sister, Marcie, who likes boys and make-up, her mother who learns foreign languages in the bathtub, and her father who goes to the office for some peace and quiet, this talkative character adds her own clever captions to the family pictures.

This amusing story is guaranteed to spark interest in writing messages on T-shirts, wall hangings, signs, and posters, and in writing captions for family pictures.

# The Reading & Writing Connection

Ask your students if they've ever had any T-shirts with printed words on them.

✳ What does your favorite T-shirt say?

✳ What does your friend's favorite T-shirt say?

✳ Does anything else in your room have a message on it?

✳ If so, what does that message say?

AFTER-READING ACTIVITIES

# Write Away

Make a copy of the message stationery on pages 82–83 for each child. Then have students cut out the pictures and try a few of the following writing activities. Tell children to write only a few words for each message.

## A Message T-Shirt

Clarice's older brother, Kurt, likes to wear T-shirts with messages on them. Ask students to imagine the kind of T-shirt Clarice Bean would wear. Have them write what her shirt would say.

## A Door Sign for Clarice

Clarice's brother Kurt has a sign hanging on his bedroom door. Ask students to imagine the kind of message Clarice Bean would hang on her bedroom door. Have them write what her door sign would say.

## A Pennant for Home

Ask students what kind of pennant they'd like to hang on their own bedroom wall. Tell children to write that pennant message.

Write a Message

# Write a Message

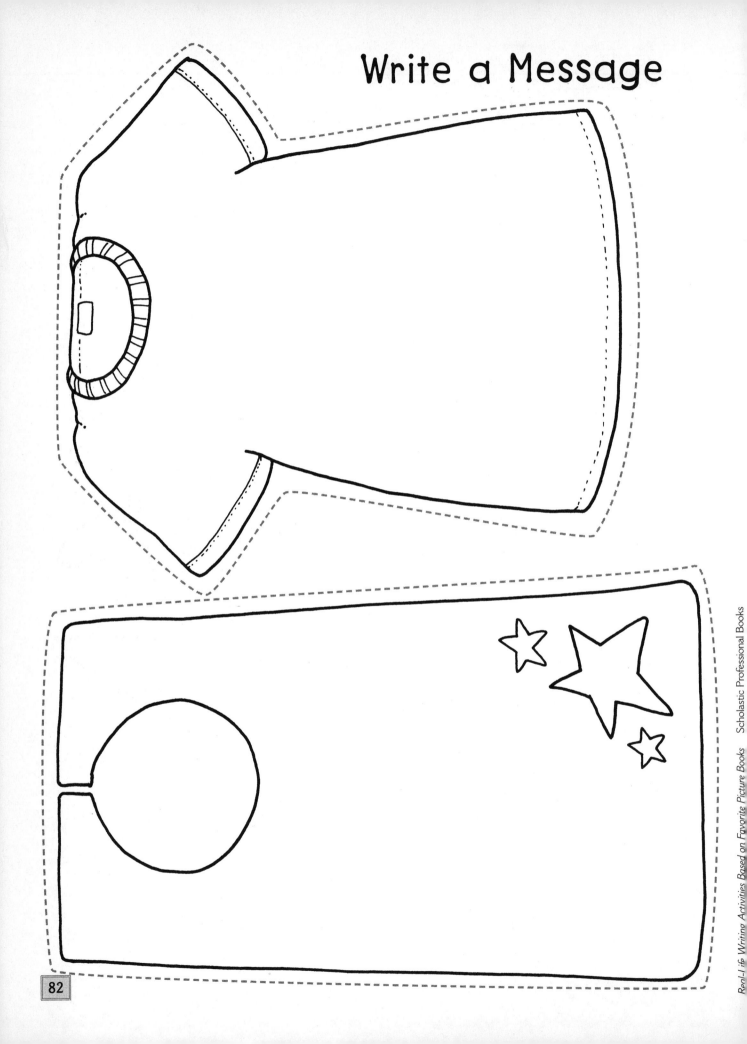

# Write a Message

## *Write Ideas*

### A Message T-Shirt

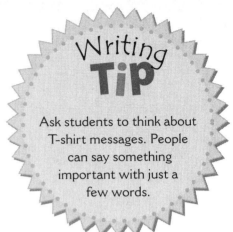

**M**ake a copy of the T-shirt pattern on page 82 for each child. Tell students to cut it out and design a favorite T-shirt. Encourage children to think of the kind of message they want on their shirt. Ask: *Are you an animal person? music lover? sports fan? traveler? Do you care about the environment? Are you against noise? pollution?* Tell them to write only a few words and add a picture.

### An E-Mail Message

**A**ll Clarice Bean wants is some peace and quiet. Make a copy of the computer pattern on page 83 for each student. Have students pretend it's Clarice Bean's computer screen and write a brief message on it. Tell them to write what they think Clarice would say.

### Family-Picture Captions

**I**nside the front and back covers of this story, Clarice Bean writes funny captions about the people in her family pictures. (She writes explanations, too.) Have students draw pictures of their families. Ask them to show each person doing what he or she likes to do best. Tell children to identify each family member by name and write an explanation like Clarice did.

# Meanwhile

By Jules Feiffer (Michael di Capua Books, HarperCollins, 1997)

Whenever Raymond is engrossed in his favorite comic book, his mother seems to need something immediately. Not in a few minutes, or later, or next Tuesday. Right then! That's when the young boy notices the word *meanwhile* printed in his comic book. "What if I had my own meanwhile?" Raymond wonders. When he quickly scrawls the word on the wall behind his bed, Raymond's exciting adventures begin.

This clever story illustrates how a few simple words can change everything. It's the perfect book to spark interest in writing everything from secret messages to messages in the sky and S.O.S. messages.

# The Reading & Writing Connection

Ask your students if they've ever written a message in the sand.

✳ What did you write?

✳ Where else have you written a message?

✳ Have you ever seen a message in the sky?

✳ What did that message say?

## Write Away

Make a copy of the message stationery on page 87 for each child. Have students cut out the pictures and try one of the following writing activities. Tell them to write each message using only a few words.

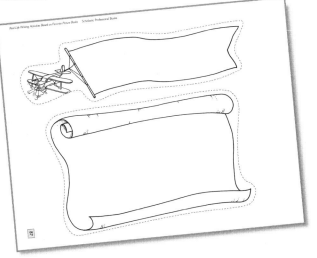

### An S.O.S.

Raymond was on a pirate ship in the middle of the high seas. He was in BIG trouble. Suppose Raymond could send an S.O.S. Have students think of the words he'd write.

### A Secret Message

Before being forced to walk the gangplank, Raymond makes a last request. He wants to write to his mother. Have students imagine what Raymond would write to his mother. Ask what kind of secret message the document might contain. Tell children to write that message and sign Raymond's name.

# Write a Message

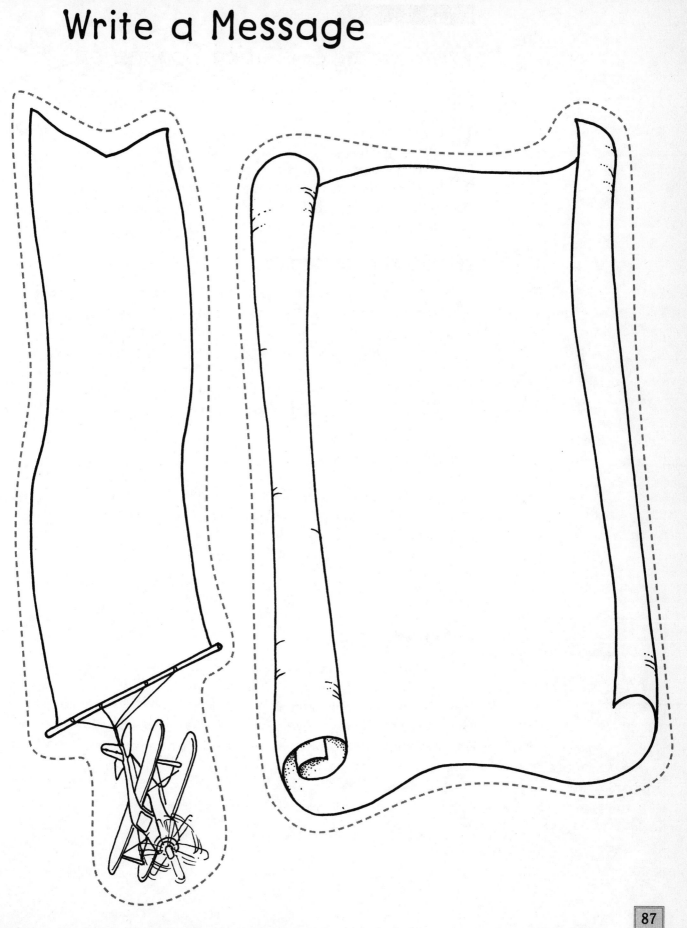

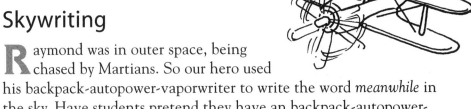

# Write Ideas

## Skywriting

Raymond was in outer space, being chased by Martians. So our hero used his backpack-autopower-vaporwriter to write the word *meanwhile* in the sky. Have students pretend they have an backpack-autopower-vaporwriter like Raymond's. Ask: *What would you write?* Have children write their important message in the sky.

## Secret-Message Art

Get ready for some finger painting. Cover a table with old newspapers and ask students to put on smocks. Set up finger paints, paper, and water. Place a blob of paint on each paper. Have students use their hands to cover a large area of paper with paint. Tell them to use one finger to write a secret message in their painting. Once read, children can make their message disappear by wiping away the message. Then they can write another message.

## A Message Board

On a small bulletin board in the classroom, post a colorful sign that reads: *Message Board*. Tack up class news, school notices, and important reminders. Encourage children to get into the habit of reading the board each day. Invite children to post their news and messages, too.

### Writing Tip

Remind students that people write messages on walls, on signs, in the sand, or in the sky. Sometimes these might even be secret messages.

---

**ANOTHER GREAT MODEL FOR WRITING**

## Mouse Practice
by Emily Arnold McCully (Arthur A. Levine Books, Scholastic Press, 1999)

Learning how to play baseball is something Monk is determined to do. Even though his parents are musicians, not athletes, this little mouse has the right idea. He's going to practice, practice, practice . . . until he's good enough to play with the big kids. This playful read-aloud could be used to spark interest in making sports banners, writing messages on T-shirts, and writing how-to's.

# Tell-A-Bunny

by Nancy Elizabeth Wallace (Winslow Press, 2000)

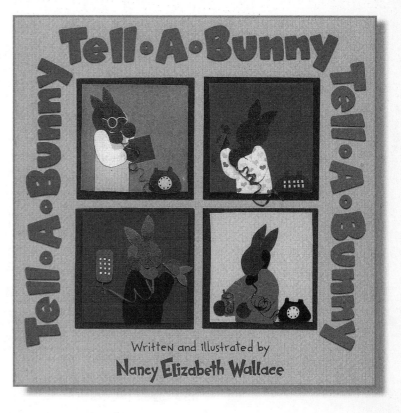

Sunny is planning a surprise birthday party for her brother, Earl, and needs some help. With her to-do list in hand, Sunny calls her friend Gloria asking her to tell the other bunnies what to bring. Gloria calls Libby. Libby calls Mugsey, and the message travels from house to house. But the message changes a bit each time it's repeated. Before you know it, the Yummy-Plummy Tan Cake becomes Yummy-Tummy Pancakes and the surprise party becomes a sunrise party. In the end, the celebration is as much of a surprise to Sunny as it is to Earl.

*Tell-A-Bunny* will remind readers of that delightful listening game Telephone in which the initial message is nothing like the one heard by the last person on the line. It's a terrific read-aloud for introducing the importance of listening carefully, writing down phone messages, and paying attention to details.

# The Reading & Writing Connection

Ask your students if they've ever taken telephone messages at home.

* \* What questions do you usually ask the caller?
* \* What information do you write down?
* \* Did you ever forget an important part of a message?
* \* Which part did you forget?

AFTER-READING ACTIVITIES

## Write Away

Make a copy of the telephone-message stationery on page 91 or 95 for each child, and have students try one of the following writing activities. Tell children to include all the important party details.

### A Telephone Message

Sunny phones Gloria about Earl's surprise party. But, Gloria doesn't listen carefully. See if students can remember exactly what Sunny said. Ask them to jot down a phone message for Gloria.

### A Bunny Message

Gloria called Libby. Libby called Mugsey. Mugsey called Baxter and Baxter called Lottie. Ask students to choose a favorite bunny and take a telephone message for that character. Remind children to tell their bunny what to bring.

# While You Were Out

**Message for:** _____

**Date:** _____

**Who called?** _____

**Phone number:** _____

**Message:** _____

_____

_____

_____

_____

**Message taken by:** _____

Real-Life Writing Activities Based on Favorite Picture Books    Scholastic Professional Books

# Write Ideas

## Telephone Game

Have players sit in a circle. Tell the first person to think of a specific message and whisper it to the person on his or her right. In turn, ask each person to whisper that message to the next player, until the last person in line repeats the message to the group. Players will have fun comparing that initial message with what was finally heard.

## Telephone Talk

Use two empty wrapping-paper rolls for telephone poles and a piece of heavy, colored yarn for the line. On a bulletin board, hang the string between the two poles as a display area for "telephone talk." Ask students to imagine phone conversations between two of the bunnies from the story. Tell them to listen in and write bunny dialogue, using quotation marks or cartoon bubbles.

## Walkie-Talkies

Have students work with a partner. Give each pair of children two small paper cups and one long piece of string. Tell them to poke a hole in the bottom of each cup, insert one end of the string in each hole, and then tie a knot inside each cup. Explain that by moving away from one another, pulling the string tight, and holding one cup to each of the partner's ears, students can have a long-distance conversation. Tell one person to talk while the other listens. Then, suggest they change places. Encourage children to jot down some scientific observations.

## Party Invitations

Have students create colorful party invitations for Earl's surprise party. Provide shiny paper, plain white paper, colored pencils, and paste for this activity. Remind children that Earl's picnic birthday supper is supposed to begin at 6:00 P.M.

## Writing Tip

Remind students that when they take a telephone message, they need to listen carefully and write down the important details. Messages need to answer these questions: *Who called? When did that person call? What did the person say?*

# Miss Alaineus: A Vocabulary Disaster

by Debra Frasier (Harcourt, Inc., 2000)

Having to miss school on Tuesday was bad enough. Having to miss school on Vocabulary Day was even worse. So, Sage telephoned her friend Star to get the list of vocabulary words for the week. Since Star was in a hurry, Sage had to listen carefully and quickly jot down the fifteen words. What happened when Sage misunderstood the last word? *Miss Alaineus: A Vocabulary Disaster.*

This amusing picture book about a fifth-grader and her vocabulary bee catastrophe will make it fun for older readers to focus on using the telephone, taking a message, asking about missed schoolwork or homework, and making a list.

# The Reading & Writing Connection

Ask your students if they've ever been absent from school for a few days.

✳ Did you call a friend from your class?

✳ Why did you call?

✳ Has a family member ever called school when you were absent?

✳ Why did he or she call the school?

# Write Away

Make a copy of the telephone-message stationery on page 91 or 95 for each child, and have students try one of the following writing activities. Have them tell who called and why.

## A Message for Sage

Suppose Star wasn't home when Sage called to get the list of vocabulary words. Someone else would have to take a message for her. Ask students to jot down that phone message for Sage.

## A Message for Mrs. Page

Suppose Mrs. Page couldn't come to the phone when Sage's mom called the school. Someone else would have to take a message for Mrs. Page. Ask students to jot down that message for Sage's teacher.

### While You Were Out

Message for: ....................................................

Date: ....................................................

Who called? ....................................................

Phone number: ....................................................

Message: ....................................................

....................................................

....................................................

....................................................

Message taken by: ....................................................

95

# While You Were Out

Message for: _____

Date: _____

Who called? _____

Phone number: _____

Message: _____

_____

_____

_____

_____

Message taken by: _____

## *Write Ideas*

### Get-Well Cards

Poor Sage had to miss four days of school due to illness. Why not make her some get-well cards? Have students browse through old magazines and cut out just the words and letters. Then have children paste some feel-good words on the outside of their cards and write a thoughtful message inside.

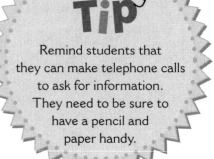

Writing Tip

Remind students that they can make telephone calls to ask for information. They need to be sure to have a pencil and paper handy.

### School Tips

Remember when Sage tells readers to follow her advice and not to get sick on Vocabulary Day? Ask students what kind of school advice they'd like to share with classmates. Have them write their words of wisdom on a slip of paper. Invite them to post that bit of advice on a School Tips bulletin board in your classroom.

### A Parade Invitation

The Webster School sends out invitations for their annual Vocabulary Parade. Have students pretend your class is planning a Vocabulary Parade next Friday at 1:00 P.M. Tell students to design an invitation for the imaginary event. Provide colored pencils, crayons, markers, and glue. Ask children to include information about who, what, where, and when.

---

**ANOTHER GREAT MODEL FOR WRITING**

## Amelia Writes Again
by Marissa Moss (American Girl, 1999)

Nine-year-old Amelia shows how much fun it is to keep a notebook. Plus, she even includes postcards, letters, messages, directions, and telephone conversations in her writing! This book will spark lots of interest in keeping journals, diaries, and more.